The Pirate Show

by Mark Landon Smith

Single copies of plays are sold for reading purposes only. The copying or duplicating of a play, or any part of play, by hand or by any other process, is an infringement of the copyright. Such infringement will be vigorously prosecuted.

Baker's Plays
7611 Sunset Blvd.
Los Angeles, CA 90042
bakersplays.com

NOTICE

This book is offered for sale at the price quoted only on the understanding that, if any additional copies of the whole or any part are necessary for its production, such additional copies will be purchased. The attention of all purchasers is directed to the following: This work is protected under the copyright laws of the United States of America, in the British Empire, including the Dominion of Canada, and all other countries adhering to the Universal Copyright Convention. Violations of the Copyright Law are punishable by fine or imprisonment, or both. The copying or duplication of this work or any part of this work, by hand or by any process, is an infringement of the copyright and will be vigorously prosecuted.

This play may not be produced by amateurs or professionals for public or private performance without first submitting application for performing rights. Royalties are due on all performances whether for charity or gain, or whether admission is charged or not Since performance of this play without the payment of the royalty fee renders anybody participating liable to severe penalties imposed by the law, anybody acting in this play should be sure, before doing so, that the royalty fee has been paid. Professional rights, reading rights, radio broadcasting, television and all mechanical rights, etc. are strictly reserved. Application for performing rights should be made directly to BAKER'S PLAYS.

No one shall commit or authorize any act or omission by which the copyright of, or the right to copyright, this play may be impaired. No one shall make any changes in this play for the purpose of production.

Publication of this play does not imply availability for performance. Both amateurs and professionals considering a production are strongly advised in their own interest to apply to Baker's Plays for written permission before starting rehearsals, advertising, or booking a theatre.

Whenever the play is produced, the author's name must be carried in all publicity, advertising and programs. Also, the following notice must appear on all printed programs, "Produced by special arrangement with Baker's Plays."

Licensing fees for *THE PIRATE SHOW* is based on a per performance rate and payable one week in advance of the production.

Please consult the Baker's Plays website at www.bakersplays.com or our current print catalogue for up to date licensing fee information.

Copyright © 2008 by Mark Landon Smith
Made in U.S.A.
All rights reserved.

THE PIRATE SHOW
ISBN 978-0-87440-187-5
#1819-B

THE PIRATE SHOW was first produced November 9, 10 & 11, 2007 by Arts Live Theatre at St. Paul's Episcopal Church, Fayetteville, Arkansas. The production was directed by Jules Taylor; set design by Garret Hunt; costumes by Faye Alter; lighting design and technical direction by Mark Andrews; Spanish translations by Mario Moreno; student assistant directors Katie Smith and Leila Sarvestani. The cast was as follows:

NIGEL HUDDERSFIELD	Cole Borgstadt
VIRGINIA HUDDERFIELD	Mary Taylor Hesterberg
MISS PERSIMMON CRUDMUDGEON	Jessica Flynn
CONSTABLE HENRY	Dylan Idlet
ALLISTER	Brian Blake
LILLIAN	Catherine Leblanc
RUTHIE	Maddy Miller
IMOGENE	Sarah Behrend-Wilcox
JAMES-LEWIS	Jordan Marshall
OPAL	Ellison Smith
LITTLE JANIE	Sierra Scarlett
CAPTAIN MAD SOPHIE MCPHEARSON	Alison Thoma
YARDARM LIZZIE	Blair Blankenship
JOLLY ELIZABETH	Megan Prettyman
SEALEGS ERIN	Katelyn Page
SCAPEGOAT ESMERELDA	Sarah Wheaton
SCALEYWAG SALLY	Becky Adams
MERRY MARTHA	Sarah Mills
MINI-MARTHA	Carly Page
CAPITAN ALBERTO ROUGHNIGHT	Zach Stolz
ALFONSO THE PARROTLESS	Austin Ross
ALBERTO SLIGHT-OF-HAND	Max Hollingshead
ALONSO THE CASH-STRAPPED	Cody Nielsen
ALEJANDRO THE BALD	Troy Squires
ARTURO SHARKBAIT	Sebastian Thomas
PRINCE PRESTON	Coleman Clark
PHYLLIS	Alexis Wilkins
PAULINE	Grace Anne Odom
PERCIVAL	Max Jardon
PAXTON	Eric Meinerding
PATIENCE	Kiana Sarvestani
PHOEBE	Kamilla Sarvestani

CHARACTERS AND SCENE BREAKDOWN

Scene One, Pgs. 5–16
PLACE: Miss Persimmon Crudmudgeon's Charm School and Orphanage For Abandoned Children

SOUND SFX: Recorded prologue at top of scene, "dream sequence"

CHARACTERS:
Virginia Huddersfield
Nigel Huddersfield
Persimmon Crudmudgeon, The Orphanage Head Mistress
The Orphans
   Alister
   Lillian
   James Lewis
   Imogene
   Opal
   *Additional Orphans may be added if needed
Constable Henry, boyfriend to Persimmon Crudmudgeon

Scene Two, Pgs. 17–37
PLACE: The London Docks

CHARACTERS:
Virginia Huddersfield
Nigel Huddersfield
Constable Henry
Persimmon Crudmudgeon
The Female Pirates Of Britain
   Captain Mad Sophie McPhearson
   Yardarm Lizzie
   Jolly Elizabeth
   Sealegs Erin
   Scapegoat Esmerelda
   *Additional Female Pirates may be added if needed
The Male Pirates Of Spain
   Capitan Alberto Roughneck
   Alfonso the Parrotless
   Alonso the Cash-Strapped
   Alejandro the Bald
   Arthuro Sharkbait
   *Additional Male Pirates may be added if needed

Scene Three, Pgs. 38–42
PLACE: The Decks of "The Pretty Penelope" and "El Bandido Loco"

SOUND SFX/MUSIC: "Ocean and seagulls"
               "Battle Music with SOUND SFX of Battle Ending

"Explosion"
"Abandon ship siren"
"Waves and Seagulls"

CHARACTERS:
Virginia Huddersfield
Nigel Huddersfield
Male Pirates
Female Pirates

Scene Four, Pgs. 43–52

PLACE: Pygmy Island

SOUND SFX/MUSIC: "Native Drums"
"Roar of a jet engine"

CHARACTERS:
Virginia Huddersfield
Nigel Huddersfield
Male Pirates
Female Pirates
Pygmy Prince Preston
Phoebe Pygmy
Paxton Pygmy
Presley Pygmy
Porter Pygmy
Patience Pygmy
Pauline Pygmy
Percival Pygmy
Phyllis Pygmy
*Additional Pygmies may be added as needed. Pygmy genders may also be changed.

Scene Five, Pgs. 53–59

PLACE: The Orphanage

SCENE ONE

"Miss Persimmon Crudmudgeon's Charm School and Orphange For Abandoned Children"

(SOUND CUE #1:

PROLOGUE:

In the darkness we hear the gentle lapping of ocean waves and the soothing call of sea gulls. In the distance a ship's bell rings followed, perhaps, by an "Ahoy, Matey!" and the screech of a parrot. Appropriate "pirate music" rises. We hear the words, "Come join me in Davey's Locker, Dearie," followed by a sinister laugh. We then hear a scream.

The lights rise on "Miss Persimmon Crudmudgeon's Charm School and Orphange For Abandoned Children," which, judging by what we see, is anything but charming. It is dismal, bleak and very Dickensian in design. The orphanage sign is weather beaten and hanging by one hinge. Inside the orphan residents are found sleeping on the floor with a lone fire to keep them warm. The scream came from **VIRGINIA HUDDERSFIELD***, a teen-aged orphan. Her brother,* **NIGEL HUDDERSFIELD***, runs to her as the other orphans wake startled.)*

NIGEL. Virginia? Are you alright? What is it?

VIRGINIA. *(Disoriented)* Oh, it's nothing, Nigel. Just…

NIGEL. What?

VIRGINIA. Just that dream… again.

NIGEL. The one about the pirates?

VIRGINIA. Yes…

ORPHAN ALISTER. Oi', what's the big idea, 'Ginia? Screamin' like that 'n wakin' us up!

ORPHAN LILLIAN. Yeah! Y'woke up haf'a London, I's suspect!

VIRGINIA. I'm awfully sorry everyone. I had a bad dream.

ORPHAN JAMES LEWIS. Was it the pirate dream again, Virginia?

NIGEL. *(Answering for her…)* Yes, it was.

(To **VIRGINIA***)*

That makes the third time this week!

ORPHAN OPAL. So's wha's 'appen in th'dream this time?

VIRGINIA. Nothing more, actually. I always seem to wake up at the same moment.

ORPHAN IMOGENE. Speaking of waking up, I hope your screaming didn't wake Miss Crudmudgeon!

ORPHAN ALISTER. Not very likely, I'd say, mate! Tha' ole Crudmudgeon hag is deep in 'er cave, eatin' rats 'n bein' smelly 'n the like.

ORPHAN IMOGENE. Does she *really* eat rats?

ORPHAN ALISTER. F' breakfast, supper 'n dinner, she does! N' y'know wha' she does after she's done eatin'?

ORPHAN IMOGENE. *(Fascinated)* No. What?

ORPHAN ALISTER. She gets up on her broom 'n flies 'igh over London, lookin' f' little girls like y'self to swoop down upon and steal to bring back 'ere to t'orphange!

*(***IMOGENE*** starts to cry.)*

NIGEL. Alister, stop it! Stop upsetting her!

(Going to console her)

It's alright, Imogene. Alister was only joking.

(To **ALISTER***, threateningly)*

Weren't you, Alister?

ORPHAN ALISTER. I was not! I've seen 'er do it m'self a 'undred times!

NIGEL. Alister!

VIRGINIA. Alister, *please*!

ORPHAN ALISTER. *(Obviously a bit smitten with* **VIRGINIA***)* Oh, alright!

(To **IMOGENE***)*

'S alright, Imogene. I's only pullin' your little legs. Tha's all. Jus' a bit 'o fun.

(To himself)

'bout *all* the fun I get 'round 'ere, I say.

(The door to the dormitory swings open as **MISS CRUDMUDGEON** *enters. A whistle dangles from her neck.* **EVERYONE** *screams and runs for whatever cover they are able to find.)*

MISS CRUDMUDGEON. Wha's all the racket in 'ere, eh? You's suppose t'be asleep, all of ya, ya buncha toads. I've a right mind t'blow this whistle 'n call m'boyfriend, the Constable 'n 'ave the lot of ye carted off to the Tower o' London where they gots them a nice dungeon with all y'names on it!

NIGEL. *(Bravely but frightened)* Miss Crudmudgeon, madam. It was Virginia. She was frightened. She had a bad dream.

*(***MISS CRUDMUDGEON*** is aghast at the gall* **NIGEL** *has to speak to her.)*

MISS CRUDMUDGEON. DID I ASK *YOU*, MISTER SCUDDERSFIELD?

NIGEL. *(Meekly)* Uh… no, ma'am, you didn't. And the name is *Hudders*field, ma'am. Not *Scudders*field. You said *Scudders*field, which is kind of funny, actually, but that's not my name. It's *Hudders*field. Not, *Scudders*field. Ma'am.

*(***MISS CRUDMUDGEON*** laughs, stunned that* **NIGEL** *continues to speak to her.)*

MISS CRUDMUDGEON. *(Sarcastically and sporting a put upon "posh" accent)* Oh…oh, I *do* beg your pardon, Sir *Mudders*field.

(She performs an exaggerated curtsy)

How very, very silly of me. I am simply mortified with embarrassment with my *terrible* faux pas. Whatever will the Duchess say?

(She suddenly gets an idea)

I know how I can remember your names, I do. I most certainly do.

Yes. How about, from this day forward, I refer to you simply as…

(Reverting to her brash, cockney accent)

…*piece of gutter trash?*

(She laughs)

Oh, yes. I like the sound of tha'. Don't you…

*(In **NIGEL**'s face)*

…*Master Guttertrash?*

VIRGINIA. Please leave him alone.

*(The **ORPHANS** gasp as **MISS CRUDMUDGEON**, once again stunned at the effrontery, turns to **VIRGINIA**.)*

NIGEL. Virginia, no!

MISS CRUDMUDGEON. Wha's this?

*(**MISS CRUDMUDGEON** approaches **VIRGINIA**.)*

MISS CRUDMUDGEON. Ah… little Miss Nightmare has found her voice, eh? Awwww…

(In baby talk)

…dwid we have us a bwad dweam? Huh? Tell Auntie Persimmon, what was you bwad dweam about, wittle one? Huh?

(Beat then menacingly)

TELL ME!

VIRGINIA. *(Inventing)* It was about our parents.

*(**MISS CRUDMUDGEON** bursts into laughter.)*

MISS CRUDMUDGEON. Y'parents!

(She laughs harder)

Y'parents!

(She continues to laugh)

Well, dearie, I'm 'ere t'tell ya the only place you two are gonna see y'parents *is* in your dreams. 'N y'know why, don't 'cha? 'Cause their dead, that's why. They died when you was jes babies and someone left y'here on m'doorstep sixteen year ago to be mother and father to ya. So here y'are. The two oldest in the orphange. 'N y'know how long ya gonna be 'here? Forever. N' y'know why? 'Cause nobody wants ya. How sad. "Boo Hoo." Y'should be grateful I put up with y'this long, coupla toads ya.

(Turning to the room)

AND THAT GOES FOR ALL OF YA!

(Beat)

I'm sick 'n tired of not bein' appreciated 'round 'ere. All I's do for ye. So I think y'should get up right now, 'n shows your appreciation for me by cleanin' this place from top t'bottom. It's a pig sty!

(No one moves.)

NOW! *MOVE!*

(Everyone scrambles and begins to clean using whatever they can find to scrub, polish and dust with.)

That's better.

(As she begins to exit)

I shall now retire to my boudoir to continue my beauty sleep.

(Beat)

AND I WANT THIS PLACE SPARKLIN' CLEAN IN THE MORNIN'!

(Beat)

AND I DON'T WANNA 'EAR A PEEP OUTTA ANY OF YOU! Y'EAR?!?

(Beat)

Buncha toads.

(She exits as **EVERYONE** *on stage continues to clean. Once they notice* **MISS CRUDMUDEGON** *is no longer in the room...)*

ORPHAN JAMES LEWIS. *(In the direction of the door through which* **MISS CRUDMUDGEON** *just exited)* "Peep!"

*(***EVERYONE** *laughs, then suddenly try to stifle their laughter for fear of being heard.)*

ORPHAN LILLIAN. If she's tryin' t'get beauty sleep, she'd better consider hibernation!

*(***EVERYONE** *stifles their laughter again.)*

ORPHAN OPAL. Yeah, 'n I bet that 'ole Tower Of London is like the Queen's Palace compared to this dump!

ORPHAN ALISTER. Hey, 'Ginia, h'come y'told old Cruddy you were dreamin' 'bout y'parents?

VIRGINIA. You heard how cruel she was when I told her I was dreaming about my parents! Imagine how cruel she'd been if I had told her I was dreaming about pirates!

NIGEL. Well, ole' Cruddy wants this place to be spic and span by morning, so we'd better get to it!

*(***EVERYONE** *continues their work until...)*

VIRGINIA. *(Uncertainly)* No.

NIGEL. What?

VIRGINIA. *(More decisively)* No!

NIGEL. Virginia, what are you talking about? Get to work. You're going to get us into trouble with Crudmudgeon!

VIRGINIA. *(With finality)* I don't care. I'm not going to do this anymore!

(Having a self realization)

I'm not going to take it anymore.

NIGEL. Virginia, what's gotten into you?

ORPHAN IMOGENE. No! I'm not going to take it anymore either!

NIGEL. Be quiet, Imogene.

(To **VIRGINIA***)*

Now look at what you've done.

VIRGINIA. What's gotten into me is the thought of being *here* for the rest of my life! *That's* what's gotten into me!

NIGEL. Come on, Virginia. Don't be a twit. It's not going to be forever. When we're adults, we'll *have* to leave. It won't be long until we're free. Just wait.

VIRGINIA. Why wait?

NIGEL. What?

VIRGINIA. *Why* wait? Let's go. *Now*!

NIGEL. You mean run away?

VIRGINIA. *(Gathering strength)* Yes. Yes! Let's run away!

ORPHAN OPAL. Yeah, let's run away!

VIRGINIA. Opal, dear, I'm afraid you *can't* run away.

ORPHAN OPAL. Why not?

VIRGINIA. Because it's not safe. You're too little. There's all kind of things out there that could hurt you.

ORPHAN OPAL. But you're going! Those things can hurt you, too!

VIRGINIA. I'm older, bigger, stronger and know a few more things. I can take care of myself.

NIGEL. Virginia, you can't be serious about this.

VIRGINIA. *(Starting to gather her few meager belongings)* I am, Nigel. I am.

NIGEL. But, like you said, there are things out there. Things that could hurt you.

VIRGINIA. I'd rather take my chances out *there*. I *know* what my chances are *here* and the odds out *there* are better!

(Beat. To **NIGEL***)*

Are you coming?

NIGEL. Virginia, I don't know.

VIRGINIA. Nigel, we've *always* stuck together. Come with me. With the two of us together, *nothing* can stop us!

(NIGEL thinks for a moment.)

NIGEL. Ok. I'LL DO IT!

(Beat)

I can't believe I'm doing this! This is *CRAZY!*

(NIGEL starts to gather his few meager belongings.)

ORPHAN IMOGENE. *(Throwing herself at VIRGINIA, crying)* NO! I don't want you to go! What'll happen to us?

ORPHANS. *(Ad libs)* "Yeah," "That's right," etc…

VIRGINIA. You will be fine. You can look after each other.

ORPHAN LILLIAN. But *you* two have always looked after us!

ORPHANS. Yeah! What are we going to do?

> *(MISS CRUDMUDGEON bursts onstage, blowing her whistle followed by her boyfriend, CONSTABLE HENRY. NIGEL and VIRGINIA make their escape as the ORPHANS adlib.)*

ORPHANS. *(Ad libbing)* "Run, Nigel," "Run, Virginia," etc.

> *(CONSTABLE HENRY chases after NIGEL and VIRGINIA as MISS CRUDMUDGEON looks on.)*

VIRGINIA. *(To the ORPHANS)* When we make our fortune we'll come back for you!

> *(MISS CRUDMUDGEON ad libs with the ORPHANS and, perhaps, calling after NIGEL and VIRGINIA.)*

MISS CRUDMUDGEON.	ORPHANS.
"They'll be dead by morning!," "You'll be dead by morning!," "'Enry, you better bring 'em back or you can get yourself a new sweetheart!," "You buncha toads, get back inside and get t'work!"	"Take care, Nigel!," "Be careful, Virginia!," etc.

(Lights fade on the Orphanage and rise on The London Docks.)

SCENE TWO

"The London Docks"

(In a continuance of the first scene, **CONSTABLE HENRY** *is chasing* **NIGEL & VIRGINIA.** *He chases them throughout the theatre, not really knowing where they are.)*

CONSTABLE HENRY. Stop! Stop you ragamuffins, I say! Stop in the name of the law!

VIRGINIA. Nigel, what are we going to do? If he catches us it's back to the Orphanage!

*(***NIGEL*** looks panicked, then gets an inspired idea.)*

NIGEL. Uh... ok... uh... ok... flap your arms like a bird. Like this. And he'll think we're seagulls.

VIRGINIA. NIGEL! Think!

NIGEL. YOU'RE the brains of this operation! I'M the muscles. *YOU* think!

*(***VIRGINIA*** thinks for a moment, then spies two barrels, placed on opposite sides of the stage.)*

VIRGINIA. Ok... uh... Barrels.

NIGEL. Uh... Rope! Virginia, this is no time to play "What Things Do You Find On A Dock!" We need to find a place to hide!

VIRGINIA. I know, seagull brain! Barrels! We can hide in the barrels! Get in!

NIGEL. Wow! Great idea!

*(***VIRGINIA*** climbs into a barrel on which is written, "The Pretty Penelope";* **NIGEL** *climbs into a barrel on which is written, "The Bandido Loco." They are unseen by* **CONSTABLE HENRY** *who breathlessly arrives at the scene.)*

CONSTABLE HENRY. *(Gasping for breath)* Ok... wherever you are. And I know you're *some*where, come out with your hands up!

(Beat)

Or don't, because I really don't care, 'cause, fish and chips am I tired!

*(***MISS CRUDMUDGEON*** enters, impatient and furious.)*

MISS CRUDMUDGEON. So, where are they, the little toads?

HENRY. Ah… Persimmon, my beautiful cup cake, I'm afraid they've given us the ole slip.

MISS CRUDMUDGEON. Given *US* the slip? You mean they've given *you* the slip. And *you'll* be lucky if I don't "accidently" give you slip right off the London Bridge, you big oaf! Where are they?

HENRY. I don't know, my bunnikins bundle! They mysteriously disappeared right before my eyes, my precious apple blossom.

MISS CRUDMUDGEON. You'll be lucky if you don't "mysteriously disappear" right before MY eyes, you big, dumb horse. They gotta be around 'eres somewhere. They couldn't 'ave gone far. C'mon, let's keep lookin'.

HENRY. What 'bout the children at the Orphanage?

MISS CRUDMUDGEON. I locked 'em up in the basement 'til I get back. The toads.

(Beat)

COME ON! SPREAD OUT!

(**MISS CRUDMUDGEON**, *followed by* **HENRY**, *exit. Once the coast is clear,* **NIGEL** *and* **VIRGINIA** *poke their heads out of their barrels.*)

NIGEL. Whew! That was close, that was!

VIRGINIA. It certainly was. Too close.

(Beat)

Nigel, we're going to have to split up.

NIGEL. Split up!

VIRGINIA. It'll make it more difficult for us to be found if we're not together.

NIGEL. But, Virginia, we've *always* been together.

VIRGINIA. It'll just be for a little while. We can split up until things have calmed down a bit, then reunite.

NIGEL. Where? When?

VIRGINIA. Well… here. On the docks. In, let's say, a fortnight. Two weeks. That should be enough time.

NIGEL. *(Fearfully)* Two weeks?

VIRGINIA. You'll be alright, Nigel. I have loads of faith in you.

NIGEL. You do? Thanks.

(Beat)

Uh… you won't forget about me? Will you?

VIRGINIA. Nigel. Of course not. It's just two weeks.

NIGEL. Still…

VIRGINIA. Uh… you won't forget about me, either, will you?

NIGEL. Virginia. Of course not. It's just two weeks.

(From offstage we hear a commotion, which interrupts.)

VIRGINIA. Someone's coming! Get down!

*(**NIGEL** and **VIRGINIA** duck into their respective barrels as a band of rowdy female pirates enter led by their captain, **CAPTAIN MAD SOPHIE MCPHEARSON**.)*

MAD SOPHIE. Avast ye hearties! Aye, I's smell that salty sea air which fills m'heart with joy, me eyes with tears and, unfortunately, wrecks havoc on me hair.

*(All of the **FEMALE PIRATES** "Arrrggg" in agreement.)*

YARDARM LIZZIE. Arrggg, Captain, yes, but what a fine day.

MAD SOPHIE. Arrggg, yes, Yardarm Lizzie, it t'was a fine day. A fine day filled with pillaging, shopping, fighting and manicures.

*(All of the **FEMALE PIRATES** "Arrrggg" in agreement.)*

JOLLY ELIZABETH. *(Who isn't very jolly; rather morose, actually)* Aye, a fine day, yes, but also a day filled with disappointment.

MAD SOPHIE. Right y'are, Jolly Elizabeth, right y'are. To think we were "this close" to the treasure map of Captain Mauvebeard and claimin' 'is treasure includin' the priceless Caribbean Ruby, until that fight broke out at The Rusty Anchor with that band of Spanish Pirates in which the map was torn in two! A map which would've led us to our fortune. Oh those dastardly…

SEALEGS ERIN. …but *really* hot…

MAD SOPHIE. …Spanish pirates!

SEALEGS ERIN. All's not lost, Captain, for I found these really cute shoes at Ye Olde Target to take away the bitter disappointment of that map thingy fiasco.

JOLLY ELIZABETH. And we do have half of the map, so we should be able to get half way there.

MAD SOPHIE. Take heart, m'lasses. All's not lost. I have come up with a plan to possess the *other* half of the map.

YARDARM LIZZIE. Oh, I *do* love a plan! I hope it involves a lot of twists and turns and a pair of panty hose to pull over our heads to disguise our identities!

MAD SOPHIE. It involves flirtation!

FEMALE PIRATES. *(Excitedly)* Oh!

MAD SOPHIE. Manipulation!

FEMALE PIRATES. *(More excitedly)* Oh!

MAD SOPHIE. Sophistication!

FEMALE PIRATES. *(Even more excitedly)* Oh!

MAD SOPHIE. And maybe… a kiss.

FEMALE PIRATES. *(Losing all self control, ad libbing, screaming and jumping up and down)* "A kiss!," "Oh, hot mama!," etc…

MAD SOPHIE. But, no panty hose.

FEMALE PIRATES. *(Disappointedly)* Oh…

MAD SOPHIE. What this plan needs is one of you lady pirates. A member of our crew who can be a coquettish little minx and flirtatiously coax the other half of this map from a member of their dastardly…

SEALEGS ERIN. …but *really* hot…

MAD SOPHIE. …crew of "The Bandido Loco."

FEMALE PIRATES. *(Shaking their fists in the direction of "The Bandido Loco" ship)* Arrrggg!

JOLLY ELIZABETH. *(Who is very morose and somber)* Pick me.

Pick me. I'm known as a man magnet. Guys really "dig" me.

(There is a moment of the other **FEMALE PIRATES** *simply staring at* **JOLLY ELIZABETH** *in total disbelief.)*

MAD SOPHIE. Sealegs Erin. I give the mission to you.

SEALEGS ERIN. Oh! Thank you, Captain! Oh, goody!

MAD SOPHIE. Alright y'scallywags, let us load our stores, board our beautiful ship, "The Pretty Penelope," and steer a course for fortune!

YARDARM LIZZIE. Batten down the hatches!

JOLLY ELIZABETH. Take in the anchor!

SCAPEGOAT ESMERELDA. Run up the mizzenmast!

SEALEGS ERIN. Take the curly q thing and run it through the thing-a-ma-bob with the what-cha- ma-call-it!

(The other **FEMALE PIRATES** *stop and stare at her, confused about what she just said.)*

SEALEGS ERIN. Oh. Uh. I actually don't know *a thing* about sailing or ships and stuff. I just joined for the travel and to meet cute guys.

(Beat)

You can borrow my hair crimper anytime you'd like.

FEMALE PIRATES. *(Cheering)* Yay!

MAD SOPHIE. *(Indicating the barrel in which* **VIRGINIA** *is hiding)* Arrrggg, Sealegs Erin, bring yon barrel with ye, won't ye?

SEALEGS ERIN. Can someone else do it? Please? I just got a mani.

MAD SOPHIE. Arrrggg! Scapegoat Esmerelda, bring yon barrel with ye, won't ye?

SCAPEGOAT ESMERELDA. *(Crossing to the barrel)* Aye, aye, Captain!

MAD SOPHIE. *(Addressing her crew as* **SCAPEGOAT ESMERELDA** *struggles with the barrel in which* **VIRGINIA** *is hidden)*
Now, you buncha lily livered landlubbers! This here voyage ain't no pleasure cruise with a midnight buffet

and bingo! No, this voyage will be one fraught with danger!

FEMALE PIRATES. Danger!

MAD SOPHIE. Peril!

FEMALE PIRATES. Peril!

MAD SOPHIE. Jeopardy!

FEMALE PIRATES. Jeopardy!

MAD SOPHIE. And perhaps the risk of your mortal souls!

FEMALE PIRATES. Mortal souls!

MAD SOPHIE. So if any of you wanna abandon ship now, like a yellow bellied coward who has a yellow belly, then step forward now.

(Pause)

MAD SOPHIE. So what's your decision, you cringin' chicken-hearted…

(Attempting to think of a word, but settling on…)

…chickens?

YARDARM LIZZIE. Captain, it's unanimous! We've all decided to… STAY!

*(The **FEMALE PIRATES** scream, hug, jump up and down as though they've just been accepted into the best sorority ever!)*

MAD SOPHIE. Then all aboard, mateys! All aboard and prepare to CAST OFF!

*(The **FEMALE PIRATES** excitedly board the "Pretty Penelope" with appropriate ad libs as **MAD SOPHIE** notices **SCAPEGOAT ESMERELDA**, who has been struggling with the barrel this entire time.)*

SCAPEGOAT ESMERELDA. Arrrggg, Captain! This here barrel seems a might heavy.

MAD SOPHIE. Yardarm Lizzie! Jolly Elizabeth! Sealegs Erin…

SEALEGS. I can't help. Manicure – remember?

MAD SOPHIE. Yardarm Lizzie! Jolly Elizabeth! Come help

Scapegoat Esmerelda with ye olde barrel!

(Grumbling, **YARDARM LIZZIE** *and* **JOLLY ELIZABETH** *cross to assist* **SCAPEGOAT ESMERELDA** *with the barrel.)*

SCAPEGOAT ESMERELDA. On three! One. Two. Three!

(THEY heave the barrel and ad libbing, load it onto "The Pretty Penelope," setting it down on the deck.)

MAD SOPHIE. And now you buncha faithhearted flibbertyjits, let's get our yellow-bellied bellys below and hatch our plot! Chip chip cherrio and all that sorta rot. *MOVE!*

(Beat)

Please?

(The **FEMALE PIRATES**, *excitedly exit "below" ad libbing about the adventure which awaits them.* **VIRGINIA** *pokes her head over the side of the barrel.)*

VIRGINIA. Pirates! And female pirates at that! Dangerous, mean and fashion challenged female pirates! I'd better make my escape whilst the coast is clear!

(Seeing all is quiet, **VIRGINIA** *cautiously climbs out of the barrel, careful to not make any noise less alerting the* **FEMALE PIRATES** *to her presence. As she tip-toes across the deck to climb down the side of the ship and to safety, we hear the* **SPANISH MALE PIRATES** *approaching ad libbing.)*

CAPTAIN ALBERTO ROUGHNIGHT. Curses on those *senoritas* of England!

(With fists thrust skyward)

Curses!

*(***VIRGINIA** *jumps back into her barrel.)*

MALE PIRATES. *(In Spanish and with fists thrust skyward) Maldiciones!*

(They simultaneously spit on the ground in a show of disgust.)

ALBERTO ROUGHNIGHT. To come so close to the Map of

Mauvebeard, which would have led us to his buried treasure and the priceless Caribbean Ruby! Only to have it ripped asunder by a buncha *chicas*! Curses!

MALE PIRATES. *(In Spanish and once again with fists thrust skyward)* Maldiciones!

(Once again they simultaneously spit on the ground in a show of disgust.)

ALBERTO ROUGHNIGHT. *Si. Maldiciones!* And thanks to those dastardly…

ALONSO THE CASH-STRAPPED. …but really hot…

ALBERTO ROUGHNIGHT. …women pirates of England, we are *still* with only one half of the map.

PEGLEG ALBERTO. We must come up with a plan to steal the other half of the map!

*(**ALBERTO ROUGHNIGHT** thinks for a moment.)*

ALBERTO ROUGHNIGHT. I'VE GOT IT! We must come up with a plan to steal the other half of the map!

MALE PIRATES. *(In Spanish)* Si! Que un plan para robar el mapa!

ALEJANDRO THE BALD. Oh, this is *so* exciting!

ALBERTO ROUGHNIGHT. But exactly… *how*?

ARTURO SHARKBAIT. I've got an idea!

ALBERTO ROUGHNIGHT. *Si*, Pirate Arturo Sharkbait?

ARTURO SHARKBAIT. I could use my considerable Spanish charm to woo the other half of the map from some unsuspecting Britsh pirate senorita from the ship "The Pretty Penelope!"

SPANISH MALE PIRATES. *(Shaking their fists in the direction of "The Pretty Penelope")* Arrrggg!

ALBERTO ROUGHNIGHT. No… no… too obvious.

SPANISH MALE PIRATES. *(Dejectedly)* Oh…

ALBERTO ROUGHNIGHT. I'VE GOT IT! Pirate Arturo Sharkbait, you could use your considerable Spanish charm to woo the other half of the map from some unsuspecting British pirate *senorita*!

SPANISH MALE PIRATES. *(Joyfully)* Ole!

ALFONSO THE PARROTLESS. *Eso es una gran idea, el capitain!*

ALBERTO ROUGHNIGHT. Yes, it *is* a great idea, Pirate Alfonso The Parrotless.

(Beat)

An idea which will take planning, timing, and considerable discussion accompanied by snacks and share time. Come! Let us board our ship, *"El Bandido Loco,"* and hatch our plot and plot our course!

*(The **MALE PIRATES** ad lib as they board their ship.)*

ALONSO THE CASH-STRAPPED. *(Noticing the barrel marked "El Bandido Loco" on the dock; the barrel in which **NIGEL** is hidden)* Capitan Roughnight?

ALBERTO ROUGHNIGHT. *Si?*

ALONSO THE CASH-STRAPPED. What about this barrel?

ALBERTO ROUGHNIGHT. *(Boarding the ship)* I see it's labeled with our ship's name, so it's obviously something we need. Bring it on board and stow it away, Pirate Alonso the Cash-Strapped!

*(**ALONSO** attempts to pick up the barrel, while the others watch, but it's too heavy. He makes another attempt and a third and final one.)*

ALONSO THE CASH-STRAPPED. Hey, guys… could I get some help here? *Por favor.*

*(The **MALE PIRATES**, except for **CAPITAN ALBERTO**, assist **ALONSO** with the barrel, which, as they are carrying it, do not notice **NIGEL**'s head peeking from over the top. They place the barrel on the deck.)*

ALBERTO ROUGHNIGHT. Good work, my friends! *El trabajo bueno mis amigos!* And now, let us retire to my quarters and devise the task before us! *Vaya! Vaya!*

*(The **MALE PIRATES**, ad libbing, exit "below." Once they have gone, **NIGEL**, sensing it's now safe, pokes his head out of his barrel. On the deck of "The Pink Penelope," **VIRGINIA** is doing the same thing. Checking if the coast is clear, they cautiously begin to exit their respective*

barrels, when they hear…)

ARTURO SHARKBAIT. *(Entering and calling after him as* **NIGEL** *hides behind something on the deck)* Si, Capitan, I will do my best and I am certain my romantic latin ways will bewitch the *senorita* British pirate to give me the other half of *el mapa*.

SEALEGS ERIN. *(Entering and calling after herself as* **VIRGINIA** *hides behind something on the deck)* Yes, Captain, I will do my best and I am certain my romantic British ways will bewitch the *senor* Spanish pirate to give me the other half of the map.

(**ARTURO** *and* **SEALEGS ERIN** *spy* **NIGEL** *and* **VIRGINIA** *at the same time.* **NIGEL** *and* **VIRGINIA** *do not acknowledge each other from their respective ships.)*

ARTURO & SEALEGS ERIN. Who are you?

NIGEL & VIRGINIA. Please, don't hurt me!

ARTURO & SEALEGS ERIN. What are you doing here?

ARTURO. Are you a… ?

SEALEGS ERIN. I think you're a…

ARTURO SEALEGS ERIN. *Capitan! Venga rapido!* Captain! Come quick!

(There is a commotion as the **MALE PIRATES** *and the* **FEMALE PIRATES** *enter ad libbing.)*

ALBERTO ROUGHNIGHT. *Que pasa?*

MAD SOPHIE. What's the matter?

ARTURO & SEALEGS ERIN. STOWAWAYS!

(The **MALE PIRATES** *and the* **FEMALE PIRATES** *gasp.)*

MAD SOPHIE. *(Approaching* **VIRGINIA***)* Well, well, well…

ALBERTO ROUGHNIGHT. *(Approaching* **NIGEL***)* …what do we have here?

MAD SOPHIE. Looks like we've got us…

ALBERTO ROUGHNIGHT. …a new crew member, *amigos*.

MAD SOPHIE. …a new crew member, ladies!

NIGEL & VIRGINIA. NO!

MALE PIRATES & FEMALE PIRATES. NO!

ALONSO THE CASH-STRAPPED. *Capitan*, we *can't* take on another crew member!

SCAPEGOAT ESMERELDA. We have just enough supplies for us!

ALBERTO ROUGHNIGHT. What choice do we have?

MAD SOPHIE. She's heard too much!

ALBERTO ROUGHNECK. He's heard too *mucho*!

MAD SOPHIE & ALBERTO ROUGHNIGHT. We'll *have* to take them with us!

ALBERTO ROUGHNIGHT. Take him below and…

ALBERTO ROUGHNIGHT & MAD SOPHIE. …throw 'em in the brig!

NIGEL & VIRGINIA. NO!

(*Beat*)

Please don't hurt me!

ALBERTO ROUGHNIGHT. *Le dolio?*

MAD SOPHIE. Hurt you?

(*The* **MALE & FEMALE PIRATES** *laugh.*)

YARDARM LIZZIE. Oh, honey, we aren't going to hurt you.

ALEJANDRO THE BALD. *Nosotros no le doldrums, mi amigo.*

VIRGINIA. You aren't? But everyone knows all pirates are mean!

NIGEL. And smelly!

VIRGINIA. And nasty!

NIGEL. And brutal!

VIRGINIA. And ugly!

NIGEL & VIRGINIA. And never call their parents!

YARDARM LIZZIE. We're none of those things.

NIGEL. You aren't?

ALEJANDRO THE BALD. Of course not, *amigo*.

VIRGINIA. But everyone knows all pirates are…

NIGEL. …mean!

VIRGINIA. And smelly!

NIGEL. And nasty!
VIRGINIA. And…
MALE PIRATES & FEMALE PIRATES. Okay! We get it!
SEALEGS ERIN. Not *all* pirates are like that!
ALFONSO THE PARROTLESS. Some *maybe*, but not us.
NIGEL. So what kind of pirates are you?
VIRGINIA. Don't you steal treasure?
MAD SOPHIE. Not exactly.
NIGEL. But I heard you talking about a treasure map, and how you need the other half.
ALBERTO ROUGHNIGHT. *Sí.* You see, the other half of that map actually belongs…
ALBERTO ROUGHNIGHT & MAD SOPHIE. …to us. But another band of pirates has it.
MAD SOPHIE. You see, earlier today we were at this great little dance place…
ARTURO SHARKBAIT. The Rusty Anchor…
SCAPEGOAT ESMERELDA. And they were having an auction for the legendary Map of Mauvebeard.
ALFONSO THE PARROTLESS & YARDARM LIZZIE. The crew of…
ALFONSO THE PARROTLESS. …"The Pretty Penelope."
YARDARM LIZZIE. …"The Bandido Loco."
ALFONSO THE PARROTLESS. …was there.
MAD SOPHIE. And we both put in, at the same time, the winning bid on the map.
ALONSO THE CASH-STRAPPED. So we both won.
SEALEGS ERIN. We tried to settle it peacefully by having a dance off.
ALBERTO ROUGHNIGHT. But suddenly everything went *loco!*
JOLLY ELIZABETH. And a fight broke out!
ALEJANDRO THE BALD. *Cuando fue hecho…*
YARDARM LIZZIE. When it was done…
ARTURO SHARKBAIT. *El mapa* was torn in *dos!*

MAD SOPHIE. Each of us came away with one half of the map.

SCAPEGOAT ESMERELDA. Here's our half.

(**SCAPEGOAT ESMERELDA** *shows* **VIRGINIA** *their half of the map, on which we can see the drawing of an island torn down the middle. On the map the letters PYG and IS are written underneath each other.*

ALFONSO THE PARROTLESS. *Aqui esta nuestra mitad.*

(**ALFONSO THE PARROTLESS** *shows* **NIGEL** *their half of the map, on which we can see the drawing of an island torn down the middle. On the map the letters MY and LAND are written underneath each other.*)

SCAPEGOAT ESMERELDA. On our half is written the letters P-Y-G and underneath that, I-S.

ALFONSO THE PARROTLESS. On our half is written the letters M-Y and underneath that, L-A-N-D.

VIRGINIA. *(Reading the lettering)* "Pyg Is?" What's "Pyg Is?"

NIGEL. "My Land?' What is "My Land?"

SCAPEGOAT ESMERELDA & ALFONSO THE PARROTLESS. One half of the name of the island.

ALFONSO THE PARROTLESS. So, we don't really know where to go.

NIGEL & VIRGINIA. What happens when you get the other half of the map?

MAD SOPHIE. We set sail!

ALBERTO ROUGHNIGHT. We draw anchor!

MAD SOPHIE & ALBERTO ROUGHNIGHT. And claim our treasure!

(*The* **MALE & FEMALE PIRATES** *cheer.*)

NIGEL & VIRGINIA. What about us?

MAD SOPHIE. You, we throw…

MAD SOPHIE & ALBERTO ROUGHNIGHT. …in the brig!

NIGEL & VIRGINIA. NO!

VIRGINIA. But you just said you were *nice* pirates!

SEALEGS ERIN. We *are*!
NIGEL. But the brig!
ALEJANDRO THE BALD. The brig's the nicest place on the ship!
JOLLY ELIZABETH. Lovely view.
ALONSO THE CASH-STRAPPED. Three square meals a day!
YARDARM LIZZIE. Soft, comfortable bed!
ALFONSO THE PARROTLESS. And on Thursdays, ice cream!
NIGEL. Wow! I *love* ice cream!
VIRGINIA. It sounds *really* nice!
NIGEL. You guys *are* really nice!
MALE PIRATES. *Gracias!*
MAD SOPHIE. *We're* really nice.
ALBERTO ROUGHNIGHT. *(Handing him their half of the map)* All right, Arturo Sharkbait. Are you ready to get the other half of that map?
ARTURO SHARKBAIT. *(Saluting and placing their half of the map in his back pocket)* Si, El Capitan!
MAD SOPHIE. *(Handing her their half of the map)* Good luck, Sealegs Erin. Remember to be flirtatious and bat your eyes a lot!
SEALEGS ERIN. *(Saluting and placing their half of the map in her back pocket)* Yes, Captain. I will do my best!

(MALE PIRATES exit leading NIGEL down "below." The FEMALE PIRATES do the same with VIRGINIA as SEALEGS ERIN and ARTURO SHARKBAIT cross down to the docks.)

SEALEGS ERIN. *(Flirtatiously)* Hello.
ARTURO SHARKBAIT. *(Imitating her flirtation exactly)* Hola.
SEALEGS ERIN. *(Flirtaceously)* How are you?
ARTURO SHARKBAIT. *(Imitating her flirtation exactly)* Como estas?
SEALEGS ERIN. *(Flirtaceously)* Oh, I love your accent!
ARTURO SHARKBAIT. *Oh, adoro su acento tambien!*
SEALEGS ERIN. My name is Sealegs Erin.

ARTURO SHARKBAIT. *Me llamo Sharkbait de Arturo.*

SEALEGS ERIN. So, that your ship?

ARTURO SHARKBAIT. *Si.*

SEALEGS ERIN. I like it.

(Beat)

It's pretty.

ARTURO SHARKBAIT. *Gracias.*

(Beat)

I like your ship, too. It's... how do you say... pretty?

SEALEGS ERIN. Thanks.

ARTURO SHARKBAIT. *De nada.*

SEALEGS ERIN. *(She flips her hair)* I'm outrageously flirting with you, you know.

ARTURO SHARKBAIT. *(He flips his hair) Si.* And I, too, am outrageously flirting with you.

SEALEGS ERIN. Oh, Arturo!

ARTURO SHARKBAIT. Oh, Sealegs!

*(**ARTURO** and **SEALEGS** run toward each other in slow motion as music underscores. When the meet in the middle, they hug and each reaches back into the pocket of the other and grabs the other half of the map.)*

SEALEGS ERIN. I must go!

ARTURO SHARKBAIT. As must I.

(They start to back away from each other.)

SEALEGS ERIN. I shall never forget this moment, Adam.

ARTURO SHARKBAIT. And neither shall I, Emily.

SEALEGS ERIN. Will I ever see you again?

ARTURO SHARKBAIT. As soon as the telephone is invented, I'll call you.

SEALEGS ERIN. Goodbye, Aaron.

ARTURO SHARKBAIT. *Adios,* Ethel.

(They are each, by now, on their respective ships.)

ARTURO SHARKBAIT AND SEALEGS ERIN. *(Proudly holding up* *their newly acquired half of the map)* I'VE GOT IT!

(Excitedly and victoriously, the **MALE PIRATES** *and the* **FEMALE PIRATES** *rush on their decks.* **NIGEL** *and* **VIRGINIA** *remain "below" offstage.)*

ALEJANDRO THE BALD. Good work, Arturo!

ALONSO THE CASH-STRAPPED. *Trabajo si bueno!*

ARTURO SHARKBAIT. *Gracias!*

ALBERTO ROUGHNIGHT. Let me see the map!

*(***ARTURO SHARKBAIT** *hands his newly acquired half of the map to* **ALBERTO ROUGHNIGHT**.*)*

YARDARM LIZZIE. Great job, Sealegs Erin!

SEALEGS ERIN. Thanks!

JOLLY ELIZABETH. Did you kiss him?

SEALEGS. Ewww! No! Gross! As if.

JOLLY ELIZABETH. *I* would've kissed him.

MAD SOPHIE. Let me see the map!

*(***SEALEGS ERIN** *hands her newly acquired half of the map to* **MAD SOPHIE**.*)*

JOLLY ELIZABETH. Maybe I should go over there and kiss him.

(Unfurling their maps.)

ALBERTO ROUGHNIGHT	**SOPHIE.**
Esto es lo!	This is it!

JOLLY ELIZABETH. It wouldn't take me but a second.

*(***ALBERTO ROUGHNIGHT** *and the* **MALE PIRATES** *and* **MAD SOPHIE** *and the* **FEMALE PIRATES** *excitedly gather around their maps.* **ALBERTO** *and* **MAD SOPHIE** *look over the front of their maps, then turn them around and look on the back.)*

ALBERTO ROUGHNIGHT. Where's the rest of it?

ARTURO SHARKBAIT. The *rest* of it?

MAD SOPHIE. Yes, the rest of it! Where is it?

ALBERTO ROUGHNIGHT. Si, donde esta?

ARTURO SHARKBAIT AND SEALEGS ERIN. It's in my back pocket right here.

(At the same time they both reach for their now empty back pockets.)

ARTURO SHARKBAIT & SEALEGS ERIN. IT'S GONE!

FEMALE PIRATES. IT'S GONE?

MALE PIRATES. *Ha ido?*

*(There is a beat and then the **MALE & FEMALE PIRATES** scream.)*

MALE & FEMALE PIRATES. Aaaaahhhhhhhhh!

SCAPEGOAT ESMERELDA. What happened to it?

ALFONSO THE PARROTLESS. *Que sucedio a?*

ARTURO SHARKBAIT. *Yo no se!*

SEALEGS ERIN. I don't know! It was in my back pocket!

ARTURO SHARKBAIT. And now it's gone!

SEALEGS ERIN. *Ha ido!*

YARDARM LIZZIE. That Spanish scallywag pirate must have stolen your half when you were stealing his!

ALEJANDRO THE BALD. That British scallywag pirate must have stolen your half when you were stealing hers!

(With the realization becoming apparent to both groups, they each race to the side of their respective ships and shake their fists at the other.)

MALE & FEMALE PIRATES. Aaarrrggg!

JOLLY ELIZABETH. So now what are we gonna do?

ALONSO THE CASH-STRAPPED. Looks like we're back at square *uno*.

SCAPEGOAT ESMERELDA. Wait a second. Wait just one piratey second. Let me see that map.

ALEJANDRO THE BALD. *Permita que mi vea ese mapa.*

*(**MAD SOPHIE** hands their map to **SCAPEGOAT ESMERELDA**. **ALBERTO ROUGHNIGHT** hands their map to **ALEJANDRO**. They each take their maps and study them as they cross to the sides of their ships so they*

are facing each other.)

ALEJANDRO THE BALD. Our map. What letters were on our map?

ALFONSO THE PARROTLESS. Um… on *our* half of the map were written the letters M-Y, and underneath that, L-A-N-D. "My Land." But there's not and island called "My Land" on any of our maps.

SCAPEGOAT ESMERELDA. On *our* half of the map the letters P-Y-G and I-S were written.

YARDARM ELIZABETH. And on *this* map the letters M-Y and L-A-N-D are written.

ALONSO THE CASH-STRAPPED. And on *this* map the letters P-Y-G and I-S are written.

MAD SOPHIE. So if we put *both* parts of the map together, we'd spell…

ALBERTO ROUGHNIGHT. P-Y-G-M-Y…

JOLLY ELIZABETH. I-S-L-A-N-D.

*(There is a moment where both **PIRATE GROUPS** are trying to figure out what this spells. Suddenly, it hits both **PIRATE GROUPS** at the same time.)*

MAD SOPHIE & ALBERTO ROUGHNIGHT. The treasure is buried on…

MALE & FEMALE PIRATES. PYGMY ISLAND!

*(There is a mad flurry of activity with ad libbing from both **PIRATE GROUPS**.)*

MAD SOPHIE. Prepare to set sail!

ALBERTO ROUGHNIGHT. *Prepare para poner la vela!*

*(The sudden tremendous noise of sailing preparations bring **NIGEL** and **VIRGINIA** racing to their decks.)*

NIGEL. What's happened?

VIRGINIA. What's going on?

ALBERTO ROUGHNIGHT. We're setting sail, my boy!

NIGEL. Setting sail!

MAD SOPHIE. I hope y'got your sea legs missy, 'cause we're lible to hit some rough waters.

VIRGINIA. Rough waters? But, I can't go to sea!

MAD SOPHIE. You've got no choice, my girl!

MAD SOPHIE & ALBERTO ROUGHNIGHT. You are now a member of my crew!

VIRGINIA. How long will we be gone?

NIGEL.	**VIRGINIA.**
I'm supposed to meet my sister in two weeks!	I'm supposed to meet my brother in two weeks!

ALBERTO ROUGHNIGHT. *Dos semanas?*

SCAPEGOAT.	**ALENJANDRO THE BALD.**
You'll be lucky to be back in *three* years!	You'll be lucky to be back in *three* years!

NIGEL & VIRGINIA. NO!

MAD SOPHIE. Cast off!

ALBERTO ROUGHNIGHT. Set a course…

MAD SOPHIE & ALBERTO ROUGHNIGHT. …with quickest haste for…

MALE PIRATES & FEMALE PIRATES. PYGMY ISLAND!

(SFX: Cruise ship horn.

As the music rises the **MALE PIRATES** *and* **FEMALE PIRATES** *gather at their rails and throw streamers, wave and ad libs "goodbyes" as though they are embarking upon a luxury Caribbean cruise.* **NIGEL** *and* **VIRGINIA** *remain in the back, unseen by each other, shocked by their predicament.)*

SCENE THREE

On the Deck of "The Pretty Penelope" and "The Bandido Loco"

(SOUND SFX: Ocean and Seagulls

As the lights rise and the music fades, we see **VIRGINIA** *has quick changed into "pirate" clothing. She stands at the rail looking longingly into the ocean.* **MAD SOPHIE** *enters from "below" and crosses to her. She stands beside* **VIRGINIA** *joining her looking out at the ocean. On the front of the ship stands* **YARDARM LIZZIE** *with a telescope scanning the horizon.)*

MAD SOPHIE. She's magnificent, isn't she?

VIRGINIA. Aye, Cap'n. She is.

MAD SOPHIE. A vast sea. Just like a big, vast… sea.

(Beat)

I've been meanin' to congratulate you.

VIRGINIA. Congratulate me?

MAD SOPHIE. Aye. You've come a long way, lass. In the three weeks since we've left London for Pygmy Island, you've become quite the pirate.

VIRGINIA. Thank you, Cap'n.

MAD SOPHIE. You've learned our ways. Our customs. Our way of talkin'. You've eaten our food. You've become an excellent swordswoman. You've learned about the sea and our ship, "The Pretty Penelope." You've adopted the "pirate look." Even adopted a pirate name, "Hayley Knifenose."

(Beat)

You've learned about the creatures of the sea. How to chart a course by the stars. How to rig a sail 'n sail a rig.

*(**VIRGINIA** siles appreciatively)*

You've learned how t'swab the decks. How t'lub the land. How t'spare the spar 'n spear the gar. You've learned how to…

VIRGINIA. *(Interrupting and irritated)* Yes. Yes, Cap'n. I've learned a great deal.

MAD SOPHIE. And even though we are racin' "The Bandido Loco" for Pygmy Island 'n anticipatin' bein' the recipients of a large buried booty, I sense somethin' is troublin' ye, Pirate Hayley Knifenose. Aye. Somethin' is troublin' ye.

VIRGINIA. Aye, Cap'n. You're mighty perceptive, y'are. I be a-missin' my brother.

MAD SOPHIE. You be a-missin' your brother?

VIRGINIA. Aye, I be a-missin' m'brother.

(Beat)

I left him behind in London. You remember. When you kidnapped me and forced me, against my will, to become a member of your crew.

MAD SOPHIE. Oh, yeah. Him.

(Beat)

Ah, chin up, Knifenose. You'll see 'im again. 'n when you do, think how rich you'll be!

*(**MAD SOPHIE** and **VIRGINIA** laugh.)*

VIRGINIA. I'd give all the money in Christendom to know he's all right.

MAD SOPHIE. Ah… sure he is Knifenose. Sure he is.

*(**MAD SOPHIE** and **VIRGINIA** remain at the rail in silence, looking out over the ocean as the waves lap the side of the "The Pretty Penelope" and the seagulls cry. The lights fade on them and rise on "The Bandido Loco" where we find **NIGEL**, who sports a pirate look, gazing out over the ocean, just as **VIRGINIA** was. On the front of the ship stands **ALONSO THE CASH-STRAPPED** with a telescope scanning the horizon. **ALBERTO ROUGH-NIGHT** enters, spies **NIGEL**, and joins him.)*

ALBERTO ROUGHNIGHT. *(Taking a deep breath)* Ahhh… smell that salt air, m'boy! There's nothing better than the smell of the ocean.

(Beat)

Except, maybe, freshly baked chocolate chip cookies.

(Beat)

Salt air and chocolate chip cookies. Nothing better than *those* two things.

(He laughs.)

ALBERTO ROUGHNIGHT. So, what's on your mind tonight, Jelly Bones Nigel?

NIGEL. What?

ALBERTO ROUGHNIGHT. Oh, well… me and the guys got together and gave you a pirate name. "Jelly Bones Nigel."

NIGEL. Why?

ALBERTO ROUGHNIGHT. Oh, well… you're a member of this crew now. You're one of our brothers…

NIGEL. No, I mean why did you chose "Jelly Bones Nigel."

ALBERTO ROUGHNIGHT. Oh, well, you're a really, *really* good dancer. Lessons?

NIGEL. *(Lost in his thoughts)* Self taught.

ALBERTO ROUGHNIGHT. Wow. I'm impressed.

(Beat)

You ok, Jelly Bones?

NIGEL. What? Oh, yeah. Yeah. I'm fine. I'm just thinking.

ALBERTO ROUGHNIGHT. About your sister?

NIGEL. Yeah. I hope she's all right. We were supposed to meet last week at the London docks and…

ALBERTO ROUGHNIGHT. I know, son. I know. And we kidnapped you.

NIGEL. She was the only family I had.

ALBERTO ROUGHNIGHT. "The only family you had?" You've got *us* now, *amigo! We're* you're family now! Why you're one of *us!* Just like you'd been with us your entire life!

NIGEL. Thank you. I mean, I really *do* appreciate it, but it's not the same.

ALBERTO ROUGHNIGHT. I know, son. I know. It's *not* the same. *But* it's all you got.

(The lights rise on "The Pretty Penelope.")

ALONSO.	**YARDARM LIZZIE.**
LAND HO!	LAND HO!

(They both slowly turn toward each other, catching each other in their telescopes.)

ALONSO YARDARM	**LIZZIE.**
SHIP HO!	SHIP HO!

*(Chaos breaks out on each ship as **MAD SOPHIE** and **ALBERTO ROUGHNIGHT** cross to ring their ship's bells to alert their crew. Both crews stumble over each other to get on deck to man their stations.)*

MAD SOPHIE. Yardarm Lizzie, bring in the topsail!

YARDARM LIZZIE. Yes, ma'am.

ALBERTO ROUGHNIGHT. What ship is that, Pirate Alonso The Cash-Strapped?

ALONSO THE CASH-STRAPPED. *(Peering through his telescope)* It's "The Pretty Penelope," Capitan.

YARDARM LIZZIE. It's "The Bandido Loco," Captain.

MAD SOPHIE. Jolly Elizabeth…

ALBERTO ROUGHNIGHT. Pirate Alfonso the Parrotless…

MAD SOPHIE & ALBERTO ROUGHNIGHT. Bring us about! Prepare to engage!

*(Bedlam breaks out on both ships as they prepare for battle. Both sets of **PIRATES** gather their arms and ammunition and assume battle stations.)*

MAD SOPHIE. Wait for it!

ALBERTO ROUGHNIGHT. Don't shoot until you see the whites of their eyes!

MAD SOPHIE. Wait for it!

ALBERTO ROUGHNIGHT MAD SOPHIE. *AHORA!* NOW!

(MUSIC: "Battle Music" with appropriate SFX including a battle ending huge explosion.

The battle rages over the heads of the audience using soft materials as both **PIRATE GROUPS** *ad lib appropriately. At some point there is a huge explosion, which signifies both ships have been hit.)*

ALBERTO ROUGHNIGHT & MAD SOPHIE. We've been hit!

SCAPEGOAT ESMERELDA. *(Looking over the side of the ship)* Cap'n… we're sinking!

ALEJANDRO THE BALD. *El Capitan, que humidos!*

ALBERTO ROUGHNIGHT. *ABANDONE EL BARCO!*

MAD SOPHIE. ABANDON SHIP!

(SOUND SFX: "Abandon ship siren"

Once again, bedlam and chaos break out on both ships. Both crews are screaming, while dashing "below deck" to gather personal belongings, which are ridiculous and anachronistic items such as hairdryers, stuffed animals, contemporary luggage, etc. Perhaps a kitchen appliance, or two.)

ALBERTO ROUGHNIGHT. *NADE PARA LA COSTA!*

MAD SOPHIE. SWIM FOR THE SHORE!

SCENE FOUR
Pygmy Island

(While explosions continue to be heard, the **PIRATES** *"swim" for the shore of PYGMY ISLAND as a sign has magically appeared among the rocks and palm trees which says, "Welcome to Pygmy Island Beach. 500 Clam Fine For Littering."*

Both **PIRATE GROUPS** *struggle for shore. Exhausted, they collapse onto the "beach" attempting to catch their breath.*

Slowly the **PIRATES** *come to their senses and to their feet. They are in their respective pirate groups stage right and stage left, squaring off.)*

ALBERTO ROUGHNIGHT. Well, as I live and breathe, if it isn't *Senorita Capitan* Pirate Mad Sophie of the vessel, "The Pretty Penelope"!

MAD SOPHIE. Well, as I barely live and struggle to catch my breath, if it isn't Captain Senor Alberto Roughnight of the vessel "The Bandido Loco"!

ALBERTO ROUGHNIGHT. *Aye, es un pequeno mundo.*

MAD SOPHIE. Aye, 'tis a small world. What's a pirate like you doin' on an island like this?

ALBERTO ROUGHNIGHT. Looking for buried treasure and the Caribbean Ruby. The same thing you're doing here, I suspect.

MAD SOPHIE. *(Approaching* **ALBERTO ROUGHNIGHT***)* Aye, that I am, Roughnight. That I am. And I be meanin' to findin' it.

ALBERTO ROUGHNIGHT. As do I, Mad Sophie as do I. And when I do find it.

MAD SOPHIE & ALBERTO ROUGHNIGHT. I don't plan on sharin'.

MAD SOPHIE. Are you prepared to fight for it?

ALBERTO ROUGHNIGHT. *Si. We* are.

MAD SOPHIE. Then… so… be… it.

(There is a moment's hesitation as both **PIRATE GROUPS** *study each other carefully. Suddenly the battle begins which is basically nothing more than a pulling hair, slap fight, pillow fight, paper-rocks-scissors kinda of thing.*

As the **PIRATE GROUPS** *continue to fight, we hear, in the distance, the distant beat of native drums which grow louder as the fighting continues.)*

MAD SOPHIE. *(Stopping fighting)* Shhhhh… listen!
ALBERTO ROUGHNIGHT. What is it?
ALEJANDRO THE BALD. *Que es?*
SEALEGS ERIN. Native drums!
ALFONSO THE PARROTLESS. *El nativo golpetea!*

(The **PIRATES** *continue to listen, then struck with fear, they realize the source of these native drums.)*

THE FEMALE PIRATES	THE MALE PIRATES.
PYGMIES!	*PIGMEOS!*

(Panic breaks out as the **PIRATES** *scramble for places to hide which they find behind rocks, palm trees and each other. In the chaos* **NIGEL** *and* **VIRGINIA** *bump into each other.)*

VIRGINIA. NIGEL?
NIGEL. VIRGINIA?

(There is a short pause.)

NIGEL & VIRGINIA. Well, shiver me timbers!

(They hug.)

NIGEL. What are *you* doing here?
VIRGINIA. Oh, well, you know. Just hanging out. Looking for treasure. What about you? You look good! What have you been up to?
NIGEL. Well, oddly enough, pretty much the same. Traveling a bit. Also looking for treasure. Stuff. Hey, I'm a Pirate now.
VIRGINIA. No kidding! Me, too! Wow! Crazy, huh?

(Beat)

Look, I'm sorry about not meeting you like I said I would.

NIGEL. Hey, hey, hey... don't worry. I completely understand. I wasn't able to make it, either.

VIRGINIA & NIGEL. Kidnapped, y'know.

(They laugh and **MAD SOPHIE** *and* **ALBERTO ROUGHNIGHT** *come up.)*

MAD SOPHIE. Excuse me, "Hayley Knifenose"...

VIRGINIA. *(To* **NIGEL***)* My "pirate name."

MAD SOPHIE. But you seem to know this scallywag!

VIRGINIA. I certainly do! *This* is my Nigel Huddersfield, my *brother*!

(The **PIRATES** *gasp in surprise.)*

ALBERTO ROUGHNIGHT. Is this true, Jelly Bones Nigel?

NIGEL. *(To* **VIRGINIA***) My* "pirate name."

VIRGINIA. No, I totally get it. Makes sense. You're a really good dancer. Right on.

NIGEL. Yes, Capitan Alberto Roughnight. *This* is Virginia Huddersfield. My *sister*!

(The **PIRATES** *gasp in surprise.)*

ARTURO SHARKBAIT. Well, this changes everything doesn't it?

SEALEGS ERIN. It certainly does!

NIGEL & VIRGINIA. What do you mean?

ALBERTO ROUGHNIGHT. The Pirates Code of Conduct!

NIGEL. The Pirates...

VIRGINIA. ...code of...

NIGEL & VIRGINIA. conduct?

(Beat)

We've never heard of it. What is it?

(The pygmies beating their drums, enter. The **PYGMY PRINCE** *steps in.)*

PYGMY PRINCE PRESTON. The Pirate Code of Conduct is a

series of rules and regulations which pirates swear to uphold. And rule 17 dash 4 point 2 dash B states that not at anytime will a pirate of one vessel be allowed to be in conflict with a pirate an opposing vessel if said pirates are blood relations.

(**EVERYONE** *stops and stares at the* **PYGMY PRINCE** *in disbelief of the fact he knows this and is able to recite the regulation verbatim.*)

PYGMY PRINCE PRESTON. We get *a lot* of pirates here.

PERVICAL PYGMY. So, it looks like you guys have to call a truce.

PYGMY PRINCE PRESTON. Yes, that's corret, Percival Pygmy. You must call a truce.

JOLLY ELIZABETH. But what about the treasure, Captain?

ALONSO THE CASH-STRAPPED. *Si, que tal el capitan de tesoro?*

SCAPEGOAT ELIZABETH. We sailed four weeks to get here!

ALEJANDRO THE BALD. And lost our ships!

(*All of* **THE PIRATES** *ad lib their questions and concerns about the treasure.*)

PYGMY PRINCE PRESTON. Oh, yeah. The treasure. Eww. Wow. About that.

(*The* **PYGMY PRINCE** *hesitates.*)

PHYILLS PYGMY. Go ahead and tell 'em, Preston.

YARDAM LIZZIE. Tell us what?

PYGMY PRINCE PRESTON. Ok, there's no easy way to say this. We spent it.

PAULINE PYGMY. Every bit of it.

ARTURO SHARKBAIT. *You* spent *our* treasure?

PYGMY PRINCE PRESTON. Well, technically it *wasn't* yours.

PAULINE PYGMY. It was on our island.

PERCIVAL PYGMY. And we *did* find it.

PHYLLIS PYGMY. And you know what they say…

ALL OF THE PYGMIES. "Finders keepers, Losers… "

PYGMY PRINCE PRESTON. Well, are just a buncha losers…

ALFONSO THE PARROTLESS. It's *all* gone.

PAXTON PYGMY. *(Defensively)* Hey, we had a lot of stuff to build!

PHOEBE PYGMY. A mall.

PRESLEY PYGMY. With an I-MAX Theatre.

PORTER PYGMY. And those aren't cheap, mister!

PATIENCE PYGMY. A couple of nail salons. Which also had to be staffed.

PYGMY PRINCE PRESTON. *And* an airport for the tourist trade. And all of that takes money. Buckets of it.

(Beat)

Sorry.

*(There is silence as **THE PIRATES** come to grips with their failure.)*

ALEJANDRO THE BALD. So, we've completely wasted our time...

JOLLY ELIZABETH. *And* our ships.

ALEJANDRIO THE BALD & JOLLY ELIZABETH. For nothing.

MAD SOPHIE & ALBERTO ROUGHNIGHT. Sorry.

THE PIRATES. *(Ad libbing)* "Oh, no that's alright," "You didn't know," "I got a great tan," etc.

NIGEL. Hey, look, guys... this voyage wasn't a complete loss. I mean, I found my long lost sister.

VIRGINIA. And I found my long lost brother.

NIGEL. If you guys hadn't kidnapped us when we accidently found ourselves on board your pirate vessels...

VIRGINIA. Then we wouldn't have found each other. So...

NIGEL & VIRGINIA. Thanks!

*(There is no reaction from **THE PIRATES**.)*

JOLLY ELIZABETH. No offense, but I'd rather have the treasure.

PYGMY PRINCE PRESTON. Oh, well, if a little treasure would make you feel better... we do have one piece left. It's not very much, mind you. We really didn't know what to do with it, but if you want it, it's yours.

ALBERTO ROUGHNIGHT. *Gracias, no.*

MAD SOPHIE. *(Aside to* **ALBERTO ROUGHNIGHT***)* Don't be rude. They're trying to make us feel better. Take it. We can throw it away later when they aren't looking.

ALBERTO ROUGHNIGHT. Oh, all right.

(To **PRESTON**)

That's very nice of you. *Gracias.*

*(***PRESTON** *reaches behind a rock and pulls out a large red ruby. The* **PIRATES** *stare at it and slowly it dawns on them exactly what it is.)*

ARTURO SHARKBAIT. Is that… ?

SCAPEGOAT ESMERELDA. I think it is.

ALBERTO ROUGHNIGHT. *(To* **PRESTON**) Where did you get this?

PYGMY PRINCE PRESTON. It was at the bottom of that nasty, old treasure chest we dug up.

MAD SOPHIE. Mauvebeard's Treasure Chest?

PYGMY PRINCE PRESTON. Why, yes, I do seem to recall "Property of Mauvebeard" to have been written on the outside of the treasure chest in curly letters. Yes.

NIGEL. Could it be?

VIRGINIA. It is!

NIGEL & VIRGINIA. It's the…

THE PIRATES. Priceless Caribbean Ruby!

(Joyful pandemonium breaks out as the **PIRATES** *celebrate their gift.)*

JOLLY ELIZABETH. Wait…

(The **PIRATES** *continue to celebrate.)*

JOLLY ELIZABETH. WAIT!

(The **PIRATES** *continue to celebrate.)*

JOLLY ELIZABETH. WAIT!

(The **PIRATES** *stop their celebration.)*

JOLLY ELIZABETH. Has anyone stopped to consider that fact of what good this is going to do us?

SEALEGS ERIN. Jolly Elizabeth is right! Here we are stuck on this island with no way of getting off.

ALONSO THE CASH-STRAPPED. *Si,* what with our ships being unseaworthy.

ALFONSO THE PARROTLESS. So this priceless ruby is worthless.

(*The* **PIRATES** *happiness is short lived as they each realize their predicament.*)

PYGMY PRINCE PRESTON. *(To* **ALBERTO ROUGHNIGHT***)* Uh... hi there. Uh... how long did you say it took you to get here?

ALBERTO ROUGHNIGHT. Four weeks. Why?

PYGMY PERCIVAL. And all you need to do to become rich is get home with this ruby?

MAD SOPHIE. Rub it in, why don't you?

PYGMY PATIENCE. Oh, well, we can help you with that.

(*The* **PIRATES** *become excited with hope.*)

NIGEL. What? You've got a ship?

PYGMY PRINCE PRESTON. Ew. No, we don't have a ship.

(*The* **PIRATES** *are devastated.*)

PYGMY PHOEBE. But we *do* have an airplane.

SCAPEGOAT ESMERELDA. *(Confusedly)* An "airplane?"

PYGMY PHOEBE. Yes, an airplane. It's a... well, a long metal tube in which you sit and it flies, like a bird, to your destination.

MAD SOPHIE. It sounds like magic!

PYGMY PHOEBE. You said it took you four weeks to get here?

THE PIRATES. *(Ad libs)* "Yes, that's right," "About that," "I could check my calendar," etc.

PYGMY PHOEBE. Well, this metal bird can have you back in London within the hour. Let's go!

(The **PIRATES** *cheer!)*

THE PIRATES. YEAH!

PYGMY PHOEBE. Now, if you will, please follow me.

(The **PIRATES** *follow the* **PYGMIES** *out, except for* **NIGEL** *and* **VIRGINIA** *who remain behind.)*

NIGEL. Oh, Virginia, I can't believe we're going home to London!

VIRGINIA. *And* we're gonna be rich!

NIGEL. And we'll get to see our old friends at the Orphanage!

VIRGINIA. *And* we're gonna be rich!

NIGEL. We'll get to introduce our old family to our new family and become the greatest of friends.

VIRGINIA. *And* we're gonna be rich!

NIGEL. Come, Virginia, let us fly home!

VIRGINIA. Where we're gonna be *rich*!

NIGEL. And while enroute, I have a terrific idea I'd like to share with you about what to do with our share of the money!

VIRGINIA. Spend it?

NIGEL. I hope the inflight movie is good.

*(***NIGEL** *and* **VIRGINIA** *exit. In the black out we hear the roar of jet engines and music.)*

SCENE FIVE

The Orphanage

(During the blackout Pygmy Island is changed to the Orphange.

In the dark we can hear **MISS CRUDMUDGEON** *instructing her charges, her slaves.)*

MISS CRUDMUDGEON. Put some back into it, y'buncha toads! I want this floor so clean by tomorrow mornin', I'll be able to see my own reflection in it!

(As the lights rise we find the **ORPHANS**, *tiredly slaving scrubbing the floor.)*

ORPHAN IMOGENE. How many days has it been now, Allister?

ORPHAN ALLISTER. One day more when y'asked me yesterday, Imogene. Come on now. They're not comin' back.

ORPHAN IMOGENE. Yes, they are. They *promised.*

ORPHAN ALLISTER. Yeah, well, sometimes promises are broken.

MISS CRUDMUDGEON. NO TALKIN'! Shut your traps, y'bunch a toads!

(Beat)

I heard what y'were talkin' about, I did. 'Bout Nigel and Virginia and how's they comin' back for you. Well, they aren't. And y'know why? 'Cause they're dead.

*(***ORPHAN IMOGENE** *begins to cry.)*

Tha's right. Dead. Both of 'em. Run over by a lorry, they pair of 'em. M'boyfriend, the Constable told me all about it. Very bloody.

ORPHAN LILLIAN. They are *not* dead!

ORPHAN JAMES LEWIS. *(To* **MISS CRUDMUDGEON***)* You shut up! Stop saying they're dead, you cow!

(Infuriated, **MISS CRUDMUDGEON** *crosses over to* **ORPHAN JAMES LEWIS** *and raises her hand as though to strike him. Just as she does, we hear...*

NIGEL. I wouldn't do that if I were you, Cruddy.

THE ORPHANS. *(Joyfully ad libbing)* "It's Nigel!," "I knew they'd come back!," "Look, it's Virginia!," etc.

*(**MISS CRUDMUDGEON** drops her hand and looks at **NIGEL** and **VIRGINIA** in disbelief. She then quickly recovers and starts to bluff.)*

MISS CRUDMUDGEON. Well, look who came crawlin' back, would ye? I thought you's was dead, the both of ye. Or so I was hopin'. Well, yer back now, are ye? Lookin' for a hand out? Huh? I shouldn't do this, but I'm just too soft hearted for m'own good, so's yous can come back, but yer gonna work twice as hard as before, y'hear me?

NIGEL. Oh, no, I don't think so, Cruddy.

MISS CRUDMUDGEON. Tha's *Miss Crudmudgeon* t'you, you ungrateful toad! How dare y'talk t'me like that in m'own orphange!

VIRGINIA. That's where you're wrong, Cruddy. You see, it's *our* orphange now.

MISS CRUDMUDGEON. *Your* orphanage?

(She starts to laugh)

YOUR orphanage, you say?

(She continues to laugh)

Well, we'll just see about that!

*(**MISS CRUDMUDGEON** blows her whistle. Immediately her boyfriend, **CONSTABLE HENRY**, is on the scene.)*

CONSTABLE HENRY. Yes, my little sweet honey blossom of love?

MISS CRUDMUDGEON. Arrest these two impudent toads, Henry.

CONSTABLE HENRY. On what charge?

MISS CRUDMUDGEON. Fraud. And lyin'. They burst in here, threatenin' me and my beautiful children. Scarin' them with tales of how they have purchased the orphange and are goin' to throw these precious babies out on the street!

(Aside to the **OPRHANS**, hissing)

CRY, you toads!

CONSTABLE HENRY. *(To* **NIGEL** *and* **VIRGINIA***)* Wha's this? These are very serious accusations! Accusations such, that if you are found guilty, you'll rot in jail.

MISS CRUDMUDGEON. Where they should be already!

CONSTABLE HENRY. *(Sarcastically)* So, *you* now own this orphange, you say?

NIGEL. Yes, we *do* say. And so does the bank.

VIRGINIA. *(Showing* **CONSTABLE HENRY** *the deed)* And the holding company from which we purchased it.

NIGEL. *And* we have a few friends to verify our claim.

(**MAD SOPHIE** *and* **ALBERTO ROUGHNIGHT** *enter.*)

MISS CRUDMUDGEON. *(Terrified)* Pirates!

(Beat)

Henry! Arrest them!

NIGEL. You can't, Constable!

MISS CRUDMUDGEON. But they're criminals, they are.

VIRGINIA. Not any more. And don't talk to my family that way.

NIGEL. They've been given a reprieve.

VIRGINIA. By the queen herself!

NIGEL. Because of all the good they are planning to do in the community with their new found fortune.

VIRGINIA. Which is also *our* new found fortune.

NIGEL. And our first purchase was this orphange. So it gives us great pleasure to say to you, Miss Persimmon Crudmudgeon...

NIGEL & VIRGINIA. You're fired!

(The **OPRHANS** *cheer as* **MISS CRUDMUDGEON** *looks confused.)*

MISS CRUDMUDGEON. Henry?

HENRY. *(Who has been studying the deed)* It's legitimate n'we are *so* breakin' up.

THE ORPHANS. *(Cheering)* YAY!

MISS CRUDMUDGEON. But where will I go? What will I do?

(Turning on NIGEL and VIRGINIA)

So *this* is the thanks I get for carin' for you all these years! For lovin' ye and nurturin' ye!

NIGEL. Don't worry, Miss Crudmudgeon, we haven't forgotten about you.

VIRGINIA. *(Indicating to MAD SOPHIE and ALBERTO ROUGHNIGHT)* Have we?

(As they cross menacingly in to a terrified MISS CRUDMUDGEON.)

ALBERTO ROUGHNIGHT. No… not at all.

MAD SOPHIE. We've got the perfect job for you, Cruddy.

ALBERTO ROUGHNIGHT. Something right up your alley!

MAD SOPHIE. Miss Cruddy, you are now goin' to be cleanin' the crud from the toilets on our new ships.

ALBERTO ROUGHNIGHT. With a toothbrush!

MISS CRUDMUDGEON. *(As MAD SOPHIE and ALBERTO ROUGHNIGHT drag her away!)* NOOOOO!!!!

THE ORPHANS. *(Cheering)* YAY!

(The ORPHANS run up to NIGEL and VIRGINIA, smothering them in hugs.)

ORPHAN JAMES LEWIS. We missed you *so* much!

ORPHAN OPAL. We knew you'd come back. We just *knew* it!

ORPHAN LILLIAN. I can't believe you bought this orphanage.

NIGEL. We did, *but* it's no longer an orphange.

ORPHAN LILLIAN. It's not?

VIRGINIA. No, it's not. In fact, we're going to tear it down!

ORPHAN ALLISTER. Tear it down!

ORPHAN OPAL. No! Where will we go?

THE ORPHANS. *(Panicked and ad libbing)* "I've got no other place to go!," "You can't do that!," etc.

NIGEL. Whoa… whoa… calm down. Listen to us. Yes, we

are going to tear the orphange down.

VIRGINIA. But we're going to build…

ORPHAN IMOGENE. A *new* orphange?

*(The **ORPHANS** cheer in happiness with that thought.)*

THE ORPHANS. YAY!

NIGEL. No, we aren't going to build a new orphange.

*(The **ORPHANS** are devastated.)*

ORPHAN LILLIAN. What then?

VIRGINIA. *(Getting down on **ORPHAN LILLIAN**'s level)* We're going to build a home.

NIGEL. *(Joining **VIRGINIA** with **ORPHAN LILLIAN** and pulling the other **ORPHANS** with him)* For *all* of us.

ORPHAN LILLIAN. But why?

VIRGINIA. Because we love you.

NIGEL. And because we're family! The whole lot of us!

(Ad libs of joy as everyone hugs.)

The End

www.ingramcontent.com/pod-product-compliance
Lightning Source LLC
Chambersburg PA
CBHW071845290426
44109CB00017B/1932